Auntie Bertie bans Christmas,

Rescue cats save the day,

With a colourful twist!

Esther Loftus Gough

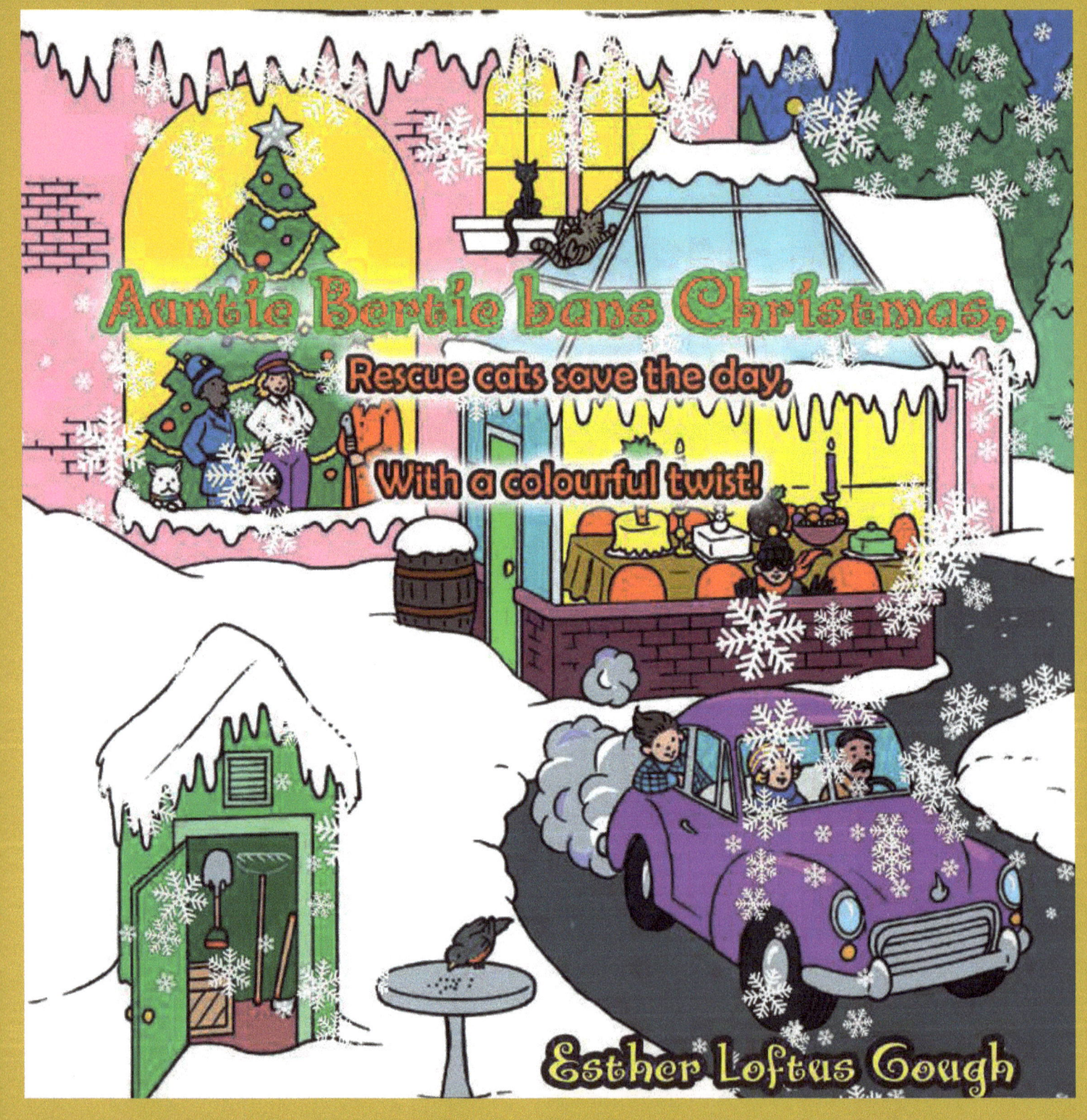

CHAPTER 1

CHRISTMAS IS BANNED

"Charity begins at home," boomed Auntie Bertie. "As it's an emergency, the children can stay with me. Mind you, they will have to be well-behaved, and as I always say, children should be seen and not heard!"

So, Auntie Bertie's nephew, Johnnie, and his friend Farah (who was always up to mischief!) came to stay for the school holidays.

Johnnie's mum, Sarah, was in hospital to have their baby, and at the same time, his dad, Tom, was meeting Farah's dad, Ash, at the airport.

Johnnie could never do anything right as far as Auntie Bertie was concerned, and Auntie Bertie was not at all amused. She shouted out in a thunderous voice, "Johnnie, you have forgotten to feed Trevor the territorial robin AGAIN, and it has started to snow. The animals and wildlife always need a helping hand."

Farah ran outside whilst shrieking, "I can do it! I can do it! I just love birds. Johnnie, come on, hurry up, we can have some fun playing in the snow and even build a snowman!"

The wooden bird table sat looking glum and empty in the snowy garden by the old apple tree. The tree looked splendid with its brown bark, peeping through the

Meanwhile, out in the old garden shed, under the plum tree by the back door, **Molly the brown Burmese rescue cat and Georgie the big, fluffy, tabby rescue cat** were cuddling up for warmth in an old wooden box. They were huddled together in a cosy, tattered old green jumper of Auntie Bertie's.

The two cats were listening in horror to the saga unfolding.

Molly sighed in her long meowing drawl. "Ooh, dearie me, I feel we are in for another eventful Christmas, or lack of it!"

In the kitchen, Auntie Bertie was spluttering and coughing. She said in a very grumpy voice, "All the birds and countryside animals need a helping hand in this cold, snowy, winter weather. Johnnie and Farah, don't you know the famous poem about the poor robin?"

"Well," thought Johnnie whilst he was patting a mound of snow together, "If we don't know it now, we soon will!"

Auntie Bertie puffed out her chest, causing her red cardigan button to ping open with the strain and her pearls around her neck to jingle jauntily. She stood at attention like a soldier on parade at the open kitchen door, as she thumped her walking stick and shuffled her feet. She spluttered out in a loud, clear voice:

"The north wind doth blow

and we shall have snow

and what shall the robin do then? Poor thing!

He'll sit in the barn,

to keep himself warm

and hide his head under his wing, poor thing!"

and hide his head under his wing, Poor thing!!

"Now secondly," shouted Auntie Bertie out of the kitchen window.

Johnnie was shuffling from foot to foot by now, looking around the snowy garden looking puzzled.

What else could he be told off for now?

Auntie Bertie sighed loudly. "Johnnie, you had a VERY bad school report, and you are far too cheeky, and you still won't brush your teeth when asked! And as for you, Farah, you seem to want to stay in bed all day listening to music. So, children, I have an announcement to make."

Auntie Bertie stood back in the cluttered, old-fashioned wooden kitchen and shouted in her loudest possible voice, "Christmas is banned! Your children's party is banned. It's not going to happen this Christmas, and if you carry on being naughty, you will be sent to bed early EVERY NIGHT!"

CHAPTER 2
NO PRESENTS?

Johnnie and Farah looked horrified.

"What? No Christmas? No party? NO PRESENTS?"

Even Susan the West Highland terrier dog ran indoors to her bed, whimpering and whining in shock.

"Auntie Bertie can be such a tyrant," whispered Johnnie under his breath to Farah.

Farah nodded in agreement, but she wanted to start building the snowman as soon as possible. Wicked! she thought with a huge grin on her face.

Auntie Bertie frowned and clapped her hands. In a loud, excited, clear voice, she shouted, "Chop, chop, I feel I cannot let all my friends down, just because I have such naughty children staying with me. I have decided to have an eggnog party, for adults only! I promised Mr. Powerplod, the local policeman, that he was invited for a Christmas-time cheery eggnog, or a glass of hot mulled wine."

Auntie Bertie loved the festive fun of mulled wine and mountains of mince pies and the loud bang of the odd Christmas cracker!

Auntie Bertie announced, "Let us start preparing!"

Meanwhile, down the lane in the snowy, ancient beamed Fox and Badger Pub, word was getting out about the Christmas eggnog party Auntie Bertie was hosting.

Also, word was getting out about her old rambling house and the fabulous gold candlesticks that would be on display in the centre of Auntie Bertie's huge cake-laden Christmas party table. The conservatory looked so sparkly and bright from the recent snowfall, and the clean, cream and gold windows gleamed with shiny candlelit icicles. The table had Auntie Bertie's prized China and her green and gold cheese holder in the centre, and it was groaning with food. In the centre stood the hugest, gooiest Christmas cake, dripping with whipped, turreted peaks of icing and decorated with a giant snowman.

Auntie Bertie loved her cakes to be different!

The red and gold velvet chairs were all in place, and the black and white tiled floor gleamed. Everything was ready for the exciting event.

Now Georgie, the tubby tabby rescue cat, had decided to follow the sun. Now he sat washing and preening himself on an upstairs window overlooking the conservatory of Auntie Bertie's house, catching the last of the day's sunshine.

Lying on his back, he lapped up the warmth. Suddenly, out of the corner of his eye, he saw movement.

Ooh, he thought, it's that cheeky territorial robin, Trevor, again. Don't know why he feels he needs to return here every year. Auntie Bertie should feed me and not him!

Suddenly, Georgie heard a very odd noise. His ears twitched and his whiskers rustled. By George , he thought, sitting up with a start. It's not Trevor the territorial robin. It sounds more like a robber, and not just any old robber. It's Roddy the robbery whiz kid from the local pub. And what's he doing in Auntie Bertie's Victorian rooftop lookout, Eyrie?

The lookout was rocking to and fro, creaking and looking very unsteady in

Georgie meowed to Molly, "Take a look at that, my Moll!"

They watched as the robbers whispered and tittered together in the

Roddy and his friend Marcie had climbed the back wall of the house using the garden shed ladder and were huddled together, planning their next move. They were determined to get hold of the candlesticks. They would sell well at the local country fair. Georgie wondered to himself, Who do they think they are—Batman?

Creeping along the red-carpet landing, the robbers tiptoed down the creaking oak staircase and crawled past the room next to the conservatory, where, by now, the party was in full swing with at least twenty guests. The guests were all fussing and patting Susan the West Highland terrier. Of course, she was loving the attention.

Suddenly, Susan's ears pricked up and she went crazy, barking at the top of her voice. Susan hadn't just heard the intruders; she had seen them creeping past the room.

How creepy!

Susan flew out of the room and skidded to a halt.

Auntie Bertie wondered what on earth was going on. "Galloping gourmets," she bawled.

The conservatory table was so heavy it was groaning with food, and the spectacular, beautiful, gleaming golden candlesticks sat in the centre.

It was very quiet. You could hear a pin drop!

The conservatory was empty of people, and the flickering candles glowed in the darkness.

The party guests were in the room next door. The noise level was booming and buzzing with laughter, jazz music, Christmas carols and merry chatter in full swing.

CHAPTER 3
THE ROBBERS STRIKE

The robbers crept into the conservatory and crawled towards the table. Roddy whispered to Marcie to keep a lookout.

Roddy crawled under the table and slipped the candlesticks into his quilted black backpack. Then he saw the cake. It stood tall and proud in the centre place, but next to it—

What was that he spied?

WOW, he spotted his favourite cake, and a massive one at that!

A CARROT CAKE.

It was sitting on the table, a huge, majestic cake with a fabulous, scrumptious array of butter icing and green leaves, with bright red butter icing carrots to top **off the display.**

"Ooh, it looks so delicious. Ooh, just one slice? Or even two? I can't resist it!" Roddy said.

Marcie whispered words of warning, "You're on a d... Stick to the plot, Roddy."

But Roddy wasn't listening. He put out his hands to grab a slice. He grabbed a huge slice of gooey carrot cake.

On the roof, Georgie was horrified. "Meow! That's my carrot cake, not his," wailed Georgie.

Georgie went wild and leapt into action, saying to Molly, "Leave this to me!"

Molly thought to herself, "I don't know about the burglar thinking he's Batman; Georgie seems to think he's batCAT!"

From the landing, Georgie sprang into action. The big, tubby tabby cat jumped from the window ledge and landed on the conservatory glass rooftop, which was piled high with a fresh, new snowfall. He started to slide and tumble and bounce down, down the soft, slippery, snowy roof.

"Charity may begin at home," howled Georgie, "but not with my carrot cake. How dare Roddy the robber take our carrot cake!"

Georgie was not bothered about the candlesticks, but Auntie Bertie would be!

Down, down Georgie skidded. He tumbled down the snowy conservatory roof, tail flying, bottom sliding, paws skidding, claws scratching.

Roddy looked up in horror. Georgie looked down with anger.

All Roddie could see was a big, fluffy tabby cat's bottom, and it was getting closer by the minute!

Panic set in and Roddy dashed for the door, tugging the backpack with one hand, and holding the gooey carrot cake in the other.

Georgie slid down the roof, getting nearer and nearer, louder and louder. **Thump, bang, crash. Roddy got more and more scared. "Great balls of fire!"** shrieked Roddy.

"Scaredy cat," meowed Georgie with the highest, loudest howl he could muster.

Roddy dashed through the door to the garden—his escape to freedom!

Georgie caught his tail on a loose tile and flew up and off the snowy roof– up, up and away into the air!

By now, Johnnie, was shouting out, "Robbers, robbers, stop the robbers!"

Farah was shouting to Susan to chase after Marcie, and Auntie Bertie was waving her walking stick in the air and yelling out, "Robbers, robbers, STOP THE ROBBERS!"

Trevor the territorial robin had heard all the fuss and was flying and swooping overhead, watching the drama unfold. "Well, I may be able to help also," tweeted Trevor. "Thanks, Auntie Bertie, for keeping me fed and watered during the winter. It's now my turn to repay you."

With a swoop of delight, the robin knocked a pine cone off the roof and it fell straight down in front of Roddy, startling him. PLOP!

Roddy looked up in amazement and stumbled. Suddenly, the hugest, biggest **ball of fluffy tabby cat was sliding up, up and away and off the roof, flying into the** air and aiming directly at him!

Or, to be more precise, at the gooey carrot cake!

Roddy screamed.

George meowed with delight and came crashing down and landed directly on the carrot cake, splattering it straight up and all over Roddy the robber's face.

"Well, that was better than any fun fair ride!" purred Georgie, who had ended up on a soft mound of snow that was on top of the wooden water barrel lid nearby. Trevor the territorial robin looked on, chuckling and chirping with amusement.

Johnnie shouted to Auntie Bertie to ask the local policeman, Mr. Powerplod, **if he had any handcuffs available.**

Soon, a muttering, bumbling Roddy the robber and his partner in crime, **Marcie, were being pulled up out of the snow and marched off and away down** the snowy driveway, and they weren't going to the local village inn, but to the local police station! Roddy was muttering and mumbling, trying to make excuses, saying that he had only wanted to have a look at the gold candlesticks.

The old police car trundled and chugged away down the drive.

Suddenly, Auntie Bertie clapped her hands. "Listen up, everyone, I have a surprise in store for you all. Roddy may be having Christmas in jail this year, but we certainly won't be!" exclaimed Auntie Bertie with delight.

"In fact, I will have the most fantastic, fabulous Christmas party tomorrow, for adults and for CHILDREN! It's party time."

"Yippee!" shouted everyone.

CHAPTER 4
PARTY DAY FUN: PRESENTS OR NOT?

It was party day!

The conservatory was buzzing with excitement; everybody wondered what surprises Auntie Bertie had in store.

Auntie Bertie was sitting, happily smiling on her red velvet seat in the corner **of the room by the warm, log fire. She was holding a glass of her very own home-**brewed favourite sweet sherry in her hand.

The roaring log fire was crackling and blazing. The Victorian gold table sat in splendour in the corner of the room, with the famous golden candlesticks glistening on top. The gold velvet tablecloth was draped over the table. Any secret surprises were hidden out of sight!

Auntie Bertie reached under the tablecloth and suddenly pulled out present after present. She shouted, "SURPRISE! SURPRISE!"

JJohnnie, Farah and Susan were all given fabulous presents by Auntie Bertie.

Johnnie unwrapped a gleaming red bike. Farah unwrapped a much-wanted violin, and Susan tore open a lovely red tartan rug.

Auntie Bertie asked, "Where are the rescue cats, Molly and Georgie? We will all have a fabulous party time together."

Molly and Georgie ran into the room, frisky and full of fun, shaking the **snow off their bristling fur.**

Georgie had been lazing in the garden. He was watching Trevor the territorial robin eat as much of the carrot cake, left in the snow, as he liked. He thought to himself with a smug smile, Well, charity does begin at home!

"Food is served, chop, chop!" boomed Auntie Bertie, clapping her hands together and shuffling along to the laden table. Shuffle, shuffle, thump, thump went her walking stick.

Under the dining room table, Molly had a plate of her favourite smoked salmon, Georgie had steak and carrot mash and Susan had her very own vegetarian garlic meatloaf.

Johnnie announced, "Hang on a minute, everyone. I will put nuts and extra bird food on Trevor the territorial robin's bird table. He needs to be fed and watered also."

Johnnie then announced he would work harder so he could protect the world from robbers like Roddy and Marcie.

Georgie, with a glint in his eye, said, "I will also work harder to prevent crimes—and get more carrot cake!"

Molly purred to Georgie not to get any more ideas; he must remember he's not batCAT!

Suddenly, a car chugged into the driveway. Out of the car stepped Sarah, Johnnie's mum, with a bundle in her arms. New baby Holly was snuggled up close to her mother.

Then Johnnie's dad, Tom, appeared holding a bundle snugly in his arms. "What, another baby? This is Theo, a brother for Johnnie."

It was the best Christmas present ever. Twins!

Farah let out a shriek of delight; her father, Ash, jumped out of the car and with a jet-lagged grin gave Farah the biggest hug.

Three surprises in one day!

Auntie Bertie clapped her hands together to make an announcement. "Now for the saviour of the day: Georgie!"

In walked a chef with a silver tray. On it was a special carrot cake, made especially for Georgie, as a thank you present for catching Roddy the robber.

Auntie Bertie said in a warm, kind voice, "Happy Christmas to everyone, and as the saying goes, charity begins at home!

Georgie, EAT UP!"

THE END

Colours can be used to aid the healing process. Visualisation and meditation are often used for relaxation. Colours are used to express feelings with mood changes often being used to express feelings.

Red blooded   Turquoise new beginnings
Orange flowing   Blue feeling depressed
Yellow bellied   Violet shrinking violet
Green with envy   Magenta sunset

Pink tickled pink - Purple with rage
White as a ghost - Silver linings
Gold - Heart of gold

Harmonising Colour Therapy

Colour can be used with opposite harmonising colour to lift the mood (as below). Colours often have an **uplifting effect.**

The eyes are the window to your soul.

Shakespeare

WARM COLOURS.	COOL COLOURS.
Red	Turquoise
Orange	Blue
Yellow	Violet
Green	Magenta

BIOGRAPHY

Esther Loftus Gough is a children's author of colour therapy books and a Book **Excellence Award finalist for** Blue in the Tooth, Teeth Hygiene with a Colour Therapy Twist!

Esther uses the power of colour to attract and hold children's attention span in her colourful, vibrant books. READ-LAUGH-LEARN! is her motto.

Esther attended the London College of Fashion and is a colour counsellor and therapist. Another Auntie Bertie adventure!

https://www.colourtherapytwist.co.uk

https://www.amazon.com/author/estherloftusgough

Also on Amazon and selected bookshops

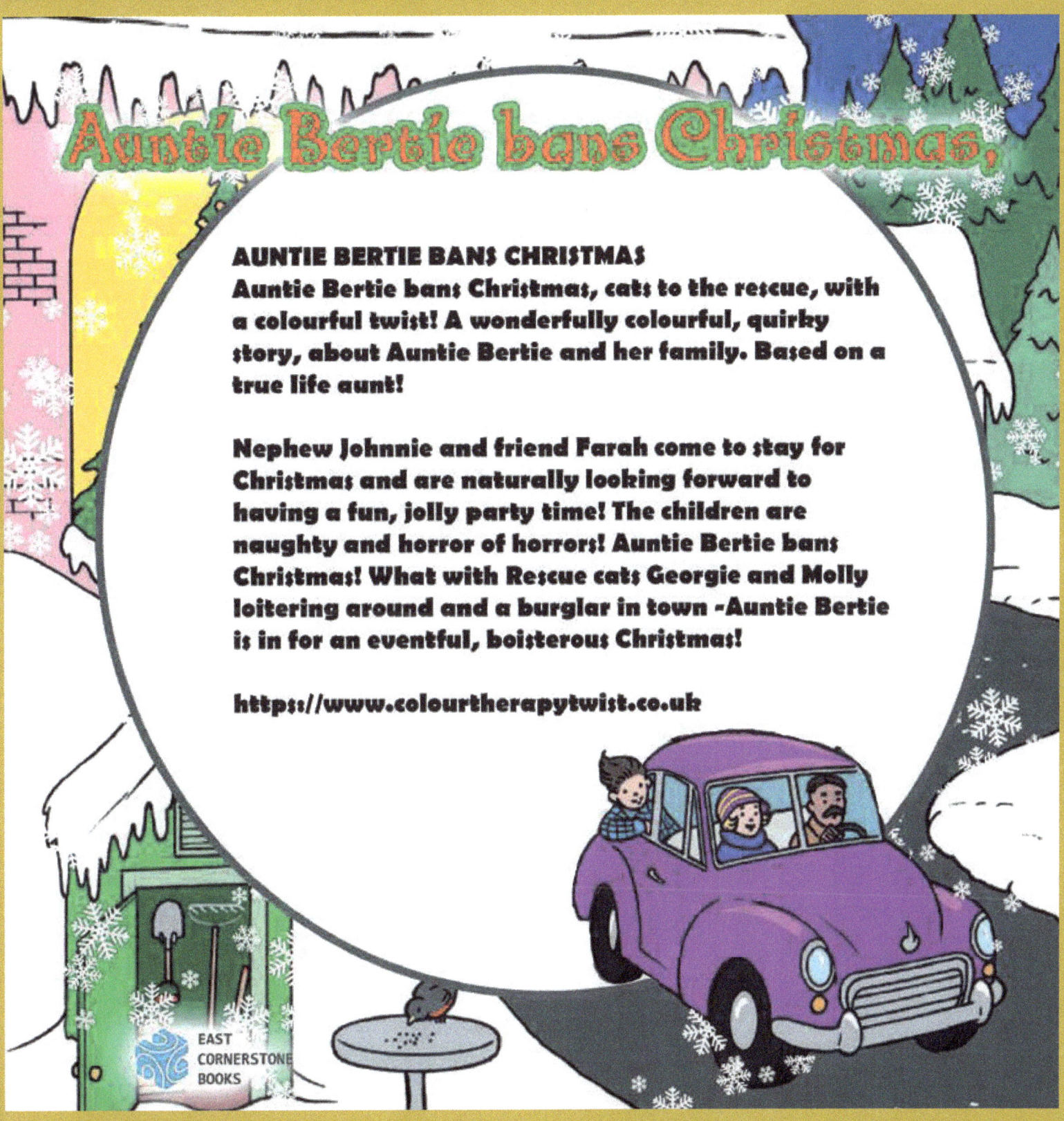

www.ingramcontent.com/pod-product-compliance
Lightning Source LLC
Chambersburg PA
CBHW040007080526
44586CB00027B/2906